CW01084564

THE SHELL OF WISDOM

THE SHELL OF WISDOM

Rosemary Anne Addison

The Book Guild Ltd
Sussex, England

First published in Great Britain in 2004 by
The Book Guild Ltd
25 High Street
Lewes, East Sussex
BN7 2LU

Typesetting in Bembo by
Keyboard Services, Luton, Bedfordshire

Printed in Great Britain by
Antony Rowe Ltd, Chippenham, Wiltshire

A catalogue record for this book is available from
The British Library

ISBN 1 85776 789 6

Blessed are you

For you are an angel,

A being of light

And of love.

You are the shell

From which will flow

Wisdom and truth.

Follow your star

In the all-embracing love.

Go where it leads you,

Always.

Don't be complicated.

Seek simplicity

In all things.

Seek the truth

And you will find it

At the heart of the matter.

Seek the juice

And you will find it

At the heart of the matter.

Listening to Love's call

Is to be open wide

To empathy,

Holding nothing back.

Being there for everyone

This is Love's call.

I am ready

I am willing

To respond

To Love's call.

I am listening to Love's call

I am listening, Love,

To Thee.

Learn to sit

Before you stand.

Learn to stand

Before you walk.

Learn to walk

Before you run.

Learn to run

Before you leap.

And thus sit, stand, walk, run and leap.

Nothing is hidden within a mystery.

So understand my silence

And you will understand my words.

I heard the call . . . . Are you listening?

I heard the voice . . . . . Are you listening?

I heard the sound . . . . . Are you listening?

I heard the murmur . . . Are you listening?

I heard the whisper . . . . Are you listening?

Then I heard nothing . . Are you listening?

I fell into nothingness.

Then I listened.

To fulfil your potential

You need to grow and develop

From within.

All changes come

From within the core

Of your being.

Look for the best in yourself.

Show a readiness to new ideas

And to thoughts as they come.

Love all

Honour all

Serve all

Value all

Nurture all

Comfort all

See the good in all.

Encourage the light within yourself

Encourage the light in others.

Become star-lit.

Move in the rhythm of the drum

Until you and the drum become one.

Cover me

Cloak me

Carry me

Into the open door of love.

The love you seek

Is as the gentleness of silence,

As snowflakes falling,

The patter of tiny feet.

The love you seek is as

The dewdrops of the morning,

The love you seek, the love you seek.

By the light you carry around you,

By the light that shines within you,

May you always be blessed,

May you be always protected.

Step into the waterfall.

Be aware of its gentle flowing through you.

Know that it has touched you at the deepest level

And that healing has taken place.

Be still, my soul.

Rest easy in thy mind.

Let light appear to thee.

Be calm and awake

To the light in thee.

I came to the door.

I opened it.

The need to hide

Was not there.

I came to offer tears of regret

But all I saw was true love.

I came to say

Forgive me, God.

But all I saw was his smile.

I came, I went

And my vision was restored.

Light my soul, O ye shining light,

Go through my whole being,

Shafts of glowing light.

Fill me with glory, O sunrise morn,

And I will be living light

And life indeed.

Shine in us

Your wondrous light of truth

Shine in us

The message of hope in you.

Shine, shine in us

Till all are one in light.

May you be blessed

And kept within love's way.

May the sun always shine upon you.

May peace share herself with you.

All you see outside of yourself

Is but a reflection,

A mirroring

Of the true self in you.

To the ebb

And flow of the sea

I lift my heart

And ask for the

Life-giving flow

That you give.

Show me the way

That I must go.

Point the way

To openness and love.

Wind, wind blow through me.

Wind, wind set me free

Wind, wind empower me,

Blessed Spirit's wind.

Every time

I walk through a forest

I feel I have grown taller

From walking

With the trees.

The stream that flows

Heals the soul.

Ripples of delight are heard.

Tis the song of a heart at rest,

The song of the soul set free.

Look at yourself in the mirror

And say

'I love you'.

You will find

A big smile will come over you.

It will make all the difference

To your day!

To keep yourself free

From all that is negative,

Let light keep open

The door of your mind,

Always.

Death is like

Going through a mist

And coming out

Into glorious sunshine.

There will never be

Enough room

To write the word "JOY".

For joy is a ripple of delight

Heard in the bubbling up of water

From the well of the heart.

The seed of life

Is already in you.

Go on your journey

With your seed

In your hand.

You can glow

In the light

If you take the flame

Within your heart.

Be as a tree

With roots

Deep in the earth.

Be as a tree

With branches spread.

Be as a tree

For all to see.

Joining is a bond

Of togetherness,

The holding of the hand

With the intention

To heal.

The feather

Falls softly

To the ground.

So remember,

Walk gently

On the land.

Take the song

Of the birds

In your heart

And become

Creation's song.

Take a cup of water,

Hand it out to the world.

Bring life to others

From the crystal stream of love.

Let love flow

As ripples across the water.

Then feel the flow

Back to you.

If you want to fly high

Set your mind and heart

In the right direction.

Remember to look for

Who you are.

Your beauty,

Your loveliness,

The love that you are.

Be the best that you can

To all people.

You will then be the best that you can

To yourself.

Above the clouds

I see you

On the rainbow trail,

Blowing shining bubbles

At the rainbow's edge.

I see a light emerging

Settling down on you,

Making you one

With the colourful rainbow.

Listen,

Not just with your ear.

Listen with your heart,

For here lies truth.

Blindness is about

Those who refuse

Not only

To accept a situation

But to see it

In the first place.

Don't ask me

To be what you are.

Just let me be

Who and what I am.

Don't ask me to change my views

In favour of your own

Or I might lose myself

Completely.

Breathe in me

Your peace and

Quietness.

So, restfully

I will go through

This day

With gentle spirit.

The acceptance

Of another human being

Is vital

To your health.